Sound Walk

Written by Charlotte Raby
and Emily Guille-Marrett
Illustrated by Susana Gurrea

Collins

6

10

11

What sounds do these things make?

After reading

Letters and Sounds: Phase 1

Word count: 0

Curriculum links: Understanding the World: The World

Early Learning Goals: Listening and attention: Listen attentively in a range of situations; Understanding: answer 'how' and 'why' questions about their experiences and in response to stories or events.

Developing fluency

- Encourage your child to hold the book and to turn the pages.
- Look at each of the scenes together and encourage them to talk about what they see and what sounds those items or actions make.

Phonic practice

- Choose one of the scenes. Make the sound of one of the things in the picture and ask your child to name what it is. e.g. 'meiow' (cat), 'waaaaa' (baby), 'tick tock' (clock). Now ask your child to have a turn, perhaps using a different scene.
- Say the sounds in the words below.
  b/u/s bus   v/a/n van   d/o/g dog   h/a/t hat
- Ask your child to repeat the sounds and then say the word.

Extending vocabulary

Look at the pictures on pages 14–15 together. Ask your child:

- Can you name each thing?
- What sound does each thing make?
- Where would you find each thing?

Now look at some of the other scenes. Ask your child:

- Can you tell me the names of the things that appear in pictures across the bottom of the page?
- What else can you name in the picture?